MW01298167

Ticket to Earth and Back

Anna Camilla Kupka

Translated from the German original
"Ticket zur Erde und zurück" (2nd edition)
Robert Betz Verlag, September 2012
ISBN 978-3-942581-39-4

Illustrations: Sylvia Gruber
Translation: Anna Drago
Editor: Doreen Zeitvogel

Copyright © 2014 by Anna Kupka
All rights reserved

Dedicated to

The Joy of Life

The little spirit is indulging in his favorite pastime. He's sitting on the edge of a silvery white feathery cloud, blissfully observing the hustle and bustle on earth. To him, it looks silly—silly and colorful, but utterly endearing.

He especially loves the oceans, the mountains, and the lakes. He can never get enough of them—how they change their color and form, whether they're draped in clouds, lashed by storms, covered with snow, or radiant with sunshine. How they adapt to the storm without struggle, or breathe in the sun's rays—and always so dignified, so noble and calm. The little spirit never gets tired of this tremendous spectacle.

And then there are the people. Sometimes they do such wonderful things that it strikes him to the core! When a mother takes her newborn in her arms, tenderly promising protection, then the little spirit sees a spark from the Mother Spirit shining through her. Or when people laugh and are happy, then each and every one of them is so beautiful that no ocean, no lake, and no mountain can compare. Oh, how the little spirit would love to always look into joyful, laughing hearts! But sadly, too often people let dark clouds overshadow their hearts and bathe them in sadness and fear. These aren't the same clouds that drift across the oceans, mountains, and lakes, covering the sun for a moment. No, it's the people themselves who conjure up these clouds through thoughts of fear and worry, and these pour down like toxic rain upon their hearts.

But why would they do something they don't like and that isn't good for them? The little spirit doesn't understand. After all, he only plays when he feels like it and it's fun—nothing else makes sense! And people always seem worried that something bad will happen. But the little spirit knows for sure they don't need to worry. The Mother Spirit protects them—nothing bad could ever happen to them. Just as they could never fall off the earth, in the same way, nothing bad could ever happen. Below, the earth is the boundary, and above, there are no limits. That's where you reach heaven, and everyone will come here sooner or later—the Mother Spirit makes no distinctions there. And to say it's bad here... no one can really claim that! Heaven is pure bliss! If you took all the shoes and purses in the world, which are so important to female humans, and if you took all the football goals and the fastest cars, which mean so much to male humans—all this together a thousand times over and over again, you still wouldn't come close to what heaven is like. Not even close! In heaven, there are no problems. All is love, and all is abundance, with enough for everyone—and much more. Still, it's never boring. Everyone is perfectly happy.

While the little spirit is pondering all this, oblivious to everything around him, he hears the voice of the Mother Spirit calling him.

"Little spirit, I have something to tell you."

"What's up?" asks the little spirit.

"It's time," says the Mother Spirit, "for you to embark on a journey."

"Time?" asks the little spirit. "I thought we didn't use that word here. And a journey? You want me to go on an adventure? I'm all ears, Mother Spirit!"

"Well, then listen closely, little spirit. The better you remember what I tell you now, the happier your journey will be. It will be an adventure—a very big adventure with you as the hero in the lead role. There will be many times when you don't feel like a hero, and like every real hero, you will go through highs and lows. But you will still always be at the heart of things, and I can already promise you a happy ending.

I think you already know what I'm saying—I can see it in your sparkle. Yes, I'm going to send you to earth to take on human form. In me and in you, little spirit, just as in every little spirit, all elements unite in infinite Love. We exist in peace, perfection, and eternal glory. But here in heaven, it's impossible for you to experience all aspects of existence, since you yourself, born out of me, are the source and the cause. On earth, however, you will experience the great adventure of discovering the different elements of your existence in all their variety. This is what we call life. You can compare it to a colorful bouquet of flowers. Until now, you have perceived the bouquet as a whole, but in human form, for the first time you will understand the uniqueness and beauty of every single flower. Each will reveal itself to you, blossom, and wither, its scent at times of tantalizing beauty, at times awakening sadness within you. Every once in a while, you will prick yourself on the thorns of a flower. The most beautiful of them have thorns, and if you can manage not to see these thorns as obstacles to turn away from but to use them as steps on a ladder leading up to the blossom—if at times you're willing to accept the pain they bring—you will finally reach the blossom and bathe in the fullness of its perfume. The thorns will soon be forgotten, for the heart prefers to open itself to happiness and joy, embracing them in love.

You were right when you said we don't talk about time here and that it has no meaning for us. For us, there is only the one wonderful moment, the Now in all its abundance—the only moment that is forever vibrant, that is true, that is alive. Where you're going, though, people not only speak of time but, if you're not mindful and stay in the Now, time will determine and regulate your entire existence. You will then be torn from your center and waver backwards and forwards between past and future. If instead of looking up toward the blossom, you wallow in the past or fearfully await the future, you will cling fast to the flower's stem as it rocks violently back and forth and makes you lose sight of your orientation and goal. Or you will hang from the stem, petrified, unable to move further.

The present moment, though, carries within it everything you need to continue climbing steadily, without rushing, becoming more and more filled with the flower's fragrance and enjoying every facet of the journey. Don't forget, little spirit, that humans are very powerful. Wherever they direct their attention is where they move. Each one of them has the power to create a paradise—a paradise full of flowers. But anxious thoughts make them forget the infinite possibilities I have given every one of my children to take with them on their way.

Every human being, without exception, is a boundless creator. They are all my beloved, magnificent children, and a part of me is in each and every one of them—in the form of you, my dear little spirit. You are my unchanging nature in every human being. And just like every little spirit, you want to play and create and delight in your manifold marvelous creations. In human form, you will want to form thoughts, see them turn into feelings, and watch them manifest in your body. And always, without rushing, you will want to keep creating and dissolving old patterns, exchanging them for new ones and forever coming closer and closer to love. May your creations and your life be a unique and captivating dance—a dance led by music that lovingly captures every tone, letting it soar and fade away, well knowing that a captivating melody is composed of different notes, of highs and lows, and does not seek to rigidly limit itself to just a few. And just as we know that every musical piece eventually ends in silence—a silence that is sacred—so you must know, little spirit, that every life will end in you, returning to you and finally to me. And even though life may sometimes lead to sorrow and to tears, perhaps even to fear, even they wish to be embraced in love. For all life, in whatever form, comes from you and me, the source of pure Love, and will return to us.

If people only remembered that everything is connected, perpetually vibrating and transforming itself, and that you, little spirit, are their innermost unchanging nature, they could enjoy all aspects of their creations in the certainty of their eternal sanctity. Then they would have the courage to play with their creations, to enjoy them, to experiment with them like a child with its toy. Then life would be the joy I intended it to be.

But sadly, life on earth still looks quite different. At night, people lay themselves down to sleep. Oh, how my heart would dance, if after a day of joyful creation, they might simply glide through the night in peaceful slumber till the morning sun summoned them to a new celebration of their creations! But most of humanity falls into bed exhausted, oppressed by the burdens of the day, and hoping for a well-deserved rest.

In sleep, people are fully themselves, and they let their suppressed wishes and hopes but also their fears surface. The mind yields its control, making room for the deeper being. Sometimes people have bad dreams, and some are tormented almost every night. But in deep sleep, each one of them allows us to speak to him again and again, to be with him, to feel his heart, to hold and caress it. Some people, when they awaken, feel a deep sense of loneliness and emptiness inside. They were home, and now they feel like they've been sent back out into the cold and confusion. This frightens them. The conscious mind then takes the lead again, and as the day progresses, its busyness makes them shove their fears and insecurities to the background, dismissing them as childish.

Yet childlike behavior is exactly what I wish for my beloved children. Those who cheerfully jump out of bed in the morning, facing the day full of joy and confidence, are always aware of our loving guidance. Trusting that my love and your existence are peacefully at rest within them, they can joyfully look forward to the beauty and the infinite possibilities each new day brings. The rest of creation also heals and renews itself at night. Thus, every morning man has a flourishing garden of fresh possibilities at hand, alive and eager to be plucked, used, and charmed into being. Yet few have the courage, gained from faith, to draw from creation with both hands, over and over again—filling their bodies, their minds, and their lives with it, with laughter and a joyful heart. Never stopping but continuously drawing from it, throwing it in the air and catching it with open mouths—bathing, burrowing, showering, and refreshing themselves in the wonderful affluence of creation. Instead, most people's creativity is overshadowed by lethargy, and rather than feeling powerful and confident in the knowledge that they, too, can create their own wonderful bouquet of life by trusting in my all-embracing Love, they experience powerlessness, fatigue, and lack."

All this time, the little spirit listened with his full attention. Never before had the Mother Spirit spoken to him in such an elaborate way—it must surely be very important. But past? and future? What was that about? Of course, you could only be in the moment—there was nothing else! Everything sounded very, very complicated to the little spirit, but somehow he also thought the Mother Spirit was exaggerating a bit. The little spirit likes people, and he knows they sometimes do things he can't understand, but there's no way they could be as crazy as the Mother Spirit makes them out to be... or could they? Besides, he's so excited about his upcoming adventure that he just doesn't want to deal with such complicated things right now. Instead he shouts with overwhelming joy: "Human! I finally get to be human! How crazy, crazy, crazy! I thought you'd never ask!" And he starts bellowing his favorite song, "Yes Sir, I Can Boogie" and jumping around like a madman—which is probably meant to be a dance of joy.

"It's so nice to see your delight, little spirit," says the Mother Spirit. "You will continue feeling this way as a human, enjoying life to the fullest, as long as you can remember that you are actually a little spirit who has temporarily taken human form. But unfortunately, like most people, you will soon forget and identify yourself with your human dress. You will believe yourself to be mortal, vulnerable, and not good enough. You will strive to be perfect and forget that you already are perfect. From time to time, you will look into the sky and feel a deep longing. It is in those moments that your heart remembers us. Sometimes you will feel a quietness and peace within you, and in those moments you will be the little spirit again and fully yourself. We will always be with you, watching, guiding, and protecting you. You won't always notice or understand it, and there may even be times when you curse and hate us. Still, we will always be there beside you. But right now none of this makes sense to you. And so, little spirit, off you go on your journey to see for yourself. To you, the journey will feel long, but for us, you will be back home in a flash.

My dear little spirit, try to enjoy the journey. I mentioned love. You have seen it many times when you were watching the people on earth. Those were the moments when you so dearly wanted to be with them. 'Love' is the name that humans have given us. If you look for it and find it in yourself and in others, you will find me, and you will experience the magic of a happy life."

"Thanks for explaining, Mother Spirit," says the little spirit. Full of enthusiasm, he adds: "That might happen to other little spirits, but not to me. How could I ever forget you and my home? How could I not enjoy the adventures down there on that beautiful planet that's sometimes covered in clouds, sometimes gleaming in the sunlight, sometimes green and sometimes blue— that has mountains and lakes... Oh, how I'm looking forward to this journey, Mother Spirit! I'll send you word every day, and every time from a different place, since I want to learn as much about the Earth as possible. I'll enjoy myself with all the other little spirits in human form. We'll have adventures together, and we'll meet here again to go over everything in detail. Oh, how I've always envied the other little spirits when they came back from their journeys and knew so much about life and wanted to talk about nothing else. Don't worry about me, Mother Spirit! I won't forget my home, but I will enjoy my experience down there to the fullest. It's just too bad it'll be over so fast! Now send me down already, Mother Spirit—I can't wait anymore!"

"If only you knew, my dear little spirit…" thinks the Mother Spirit. But she says nothing, and with a smile, she sends the little spirit down to earth. "I am with you, little spirit, I am with you," she thinks, and gazes downward to follow her protégé's journey and sometimes guide him a little along the way.

The little spirit finds himself in water. It's dark, and he can detect neither mountains nor lakes. But at least it's nice and warm. He sways back and forth a little and feels pretty good. He also trusts that the Mother Spirit knows what he's doing and that everything is all right. But then he realizes that he has no body at all—at least, not the kind he's seen on human beings. He seems to be... a point. Then he remembers that the Mother Spirit is always with him, so he asks her where his body is—the one with those funny long legs and arms, and a head full of hair.

"It still has to grow," replies the Mother Spirit. "You are in the womb now, which is a part of your mother's body. You will stay there until your own body has developed enough to survive on earth. You will have nice parents. They have wanted a child for a long time, and you will be the child they have always dreamt of. They will take good care of you and only want the best for you. Not every little spirit who takes human form is born into such a loving family, but ultimately every one of you has to face your own challenges."

The little spirit is pretty upset. First of all, the Mother Spirit could easily have sent him to earth more fully developed. It surely was possible, but she obviously believed that he'd need the same time to develop as all the others. And not only that, she'd made it easier for him by sending him to a loving family and letting him be a "dream child." The Mother Spirit must think he's not strong enough to spend his childhood without a protective mommy. In heaven, those who have had a so-called difficult childhood are considered experts on human experience. Much-awaited children and pampered children are sometimes ridiculed, since everything has been made so easy for them. Yet the Mother Spirit always insists that everyone ultimately has to face the same challenges. Still, how the little spirit would love to not be a "dream child!" How he would enjoy telling everybody up in heaven about a difficult childhood and about those things they call drugs and alcohol!

He hears a loud "Ahem," which is very different from the other far-off sounds in this so-called womb. Oh, no! He totally forgot the Mother Spirit is always listening and sometimes obviously decides to intervene. The little spirit is slightly annoyed. Can't he just start the human life he's been dreaming of for so long without the Mother Spirit already interfering? "Don't worry," he can hear the Mother Spirit say with a smile in her voice. "Soon you will no longer hear me interfering. So let's enjoy this time while you're still willing to hear me. And since you have already had the human experience of being annoyed, I encourage you to also experience gratitude, especially gratitude for being born into a loving family, whose members will make it so much easier for you to recognize me."

The little spirit is already no longer sure if he really wants the Mother Spirit around all the time. He wants to have a human experience, with all its ups and downs, without being constantly monitored and protected. "Mother hen," he thinks to himself, but he thinks it very, very quietly. Not quietly enough, though, as he can tell from a barely audible laugh. OK, so there's no escape. Better start accepting things the way they are, without being at odds with his fate before his life on earth has even started. That happens enough already, as he's heard from the little spirits who've returned to heaven. And those who were seen as being smart on earth all agree that it's best to just accept things as they are. For some reason, they all seem to trust the Mother Spirit's guidance.

The little spirit would love to wrinkle his forehead, something he's often seen people do when he watched them from heaven. But he doesn't yet have a forehead he can wrinkle, so he looks around for a different way to express his disapproval—and hears a quiet chuckle. This is beginning to really annoy him, so he decides to go to sleep. And in his sleep, he secretly enjoys being back home in the Mother Spirit's arms.

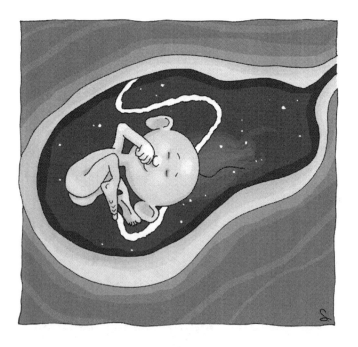

In the next few months, the little spirit's body and brain grow and develop. He's still a little disappointed that he can't yet see the mountains and lakes. But he enjoys feeling his body grow and sensing new things every day. Sometimes he finds his existence disgusting, especially when it gets too warm or his mother eats something he finds revolting. Once she drank something that at first made him want to sing "Yes Sir, I Can Boogie" again, but it soon made him so nauseous that, more than anything, he wanted to go back to heaven as fast as possible. But most of the time he shares her taste, and the day she finds out about him, she radiates so much joy he almost feels like he's back in heaven. This must be the love the Mother Spirit talked about. It feels great, and the little spirit is now secretly happy to have such loving parents. The only problem is that his mother is so careful now, since she's afraid he might decide he'd rather not come to earth after all. Before, she used to dance and laugh so hard her belly would shake and go up and down, which the little spirit really enjoyed. Now she's much calmer, but she makes up for it by listening to a lot of nice music, another thing the little spirit really enjoys. Sometimes she strokes her belly, which he can feel and he likes.

The little spirit grows and grows. The legs and arms he's so eagerly awaited are getting longer, and his head seems unbelievably huge, though still without hair. But it will grow—he knows enough to comfort himself. Now, though, he needs to figure out how to get out of this tight sack. It's gradually getting boring and really very, very cramped. But the Mother Spirit tells him he has to wait a little longer. His time will come. He now begins to understand the term "time"—everything takes so long on earth! But soon, soon he will see the mountains and lakes—he can hardly wait!

Finally, the Mother Spirit gives him the sign that it's time for him to start making his way out. His mother seems to have gotten the same signal, as suddenly everything around him starts to contract in waves and he abruptly feels pushed in one direction. Straight ahead, he can see a tiny hole—much too tiny to ever get his huge head and his long arms and legs through. This must be the wrong direction! He fights the push and looks around—where should he go? But he can't see any other opening. Now, for the first time in his short existence, he begins to feel panic—a terrible, gut-wrenching panic, beyond any horror he could ever have imagined. He can't go through this tiny hole—it can't be! He'll never fit through! He doesn't want to leave. He wants to stay where he is. There's screaming inside his head—he screams for the Mother Spirit. His heart wants to burst. He doesn't know what to do with his arms. He's frightened and in pain. But inevitably, he's pushed towards the tiny hole, farther and farther, till a narrow canal opens up before him and closes in around him. By some miracle, he fits into it, and in agony he pushes his way through it.

His mother is also suffering—he can hear her scream. He's hurting her. Now she probably no longer wants him and regrets the day she was so happy about him.

The little spirit is afraid—he's afraid of her pain, afraid of his agony, afraid to be left on earth all alone. His heart is crying out for the Mother Spirit. He doesn't want to be human anymore. But now there's no turning back. Onward and onward he goes, until he finally feels a gentle breeze on his head. Hands pull him, he struggles, and then—he's out! He's out… but the panic isn't over. This is air! How is he supposed to survive here? All he knows is water. He's going to die before he even lives! And then, the most incredible thing happens. The air starts to flow into his lungs, and he begins to wail. He didn't die. He's alive! And he starts to cry. He cries and cries and cries, and he cannot stop.

This is not how he imagined human life. He's feeling lonely. Instead of seeing the sun, he feels cold. And his body aches all over—the body he's so looked forward to. Everything feels squeezed, and it hurts. He cries and cries and wants to return to where it's warm and cozy. He wants to return to the Mother Spirit. Coldness wraps itself around his little heart, and he feels an infinite sadness within him.

But then he feels a loving embrace. Warmth flows right through him, and as he looks up, he sees his mother's gentle eyes for the first time—eyes that look at him full of love and tenderness. And behind his mother, he sees his father, who radiates peace and protection. And as he looks into his parents' trusting eyes, he knows that he'll never again need to fear being unwelcome.

But now he's tired, and all he wants to do is sleep. As he closes his eyes, he talks to the Mother Spirit. He tells her this was the most painful experience he could ever have imagined—that he isn't sure he would have chosen to be human had he known what he would have to face. On the other hand, now that he's survived the worst—what else could possibly unsettle him? And as soon as he finishes this thought, he falls into a deep, well-deserved sleep.

He still can't believe it. He's alive! He really is a human being now. But in truth, he'd imagined things a little differently. He can't talk, he can't do anything on his own, he has to constantly scream to get attention, and then his mother and father have to figure out what he wants. It's never much. He mostly just wants to drink or be held in those warm, loving arms. He loves it when they blow kisses on the back of his head and play with his legs. And he loves hearing their laughter and seeing their joy, especially since he knows that he's the reason for that joy. Then he does the same things over and over to make them laugh again. These are the good times.

But there are other times, too, like when his parents scold him because he's crying again, seemingly for no reason. Or when he keeps waking them up at night and they get more and more exhausted. Then, and only then—and he would never admit it—he sometimes quietly thinks to himself that he misses the spontaneity and joy of heaven and the boundless love he always received from the Mother Spirit and the other little spirits. No one was ever exhausted, angry, or sad, and nothing was ever lacking. Everything was available in abundance.

His mother and father are trying to do their best. The little spirit can feel it, but he can also feel their insecurity and the lack of understanding that sometimes exists between them. Sometimes he's haunted by a feeling that was inconceivable to him a few months ago. He feels homesick. He seems to understand that his life on earth will feel very long, much longer than expected. And in his short life as a human being so far, he has already experienced that human existence can be very painful.

"That's the second painful experience in such a short time," the little spirit thinks. "First, the incredible physical pain of coming into this world, and now the pain in my heart because I miss my home so much." And he starts to cry again. His mother comes and takes him in her arms. But she doesn't know why he's crying, since he's just eaten. Worried, she and his father look at each other, hoping that this is just a passing phase.

When the little spirit is alone, the Mother Spirit comes to visit him, especially when he's asleep. "Little spirit", she says, "I told you I would always be with you. Every breath connects you with me. Your earthly parents are full of love and will always do their best. You were created from love, but the human form, with all its sorrows, often overshadows the unconditional love you are used to from me. So trust that I always hold you in my arms and that within your parents, too, there lives a little spirit who has gone on the temporary journey of being human and thus also displays human weaknesses."

Whenever he hears the Mother Spirit's voice, the little spirit feels happy and secure. More and more, he can see his parent's caring efforts, and for that he loves them very much.

The little spirit develops his human abilities quickly. After all, back in heaven he couldn't wait to finally be allowed to come to earth. This isn't true of every little spirit. Many of them would rather stay in heaven instead of engaging in the toils of human life. So when the Mother Spirit sends them to earth, in silent protest they take their sweet time developing their skills. Not so our little spirit. He is full of curiosity and learns something new every day. He knows he isn't actually learning anything new, since from the beginning all possibilities are inherent in every little spirit. But it's a change for him to have to redirect his skills to his human form.

He soon crawls and takes his first steps early on. His parents are overjoyed and beam with pride. Sure, it's more work than they thought it would be, but the little spirit knows he can thrill them with his laughter and every newly learned skill. Then they forget how much trouble it is, and their laughter is so bright that he can catch sight of the little spirits within them. This makes him happy, and he greets them and almost feels like he's home again.

But there's another side, too. As wonderful as the little spirit finds the world, with all its colors and sounds, it surprises and confuses him just as much—especially since something always seems to be expected from him. He is the center of attention for his new family, and whenever people come to visit, they all rally around him. He quickly realizes that they expect him to not cry but to do things that make the people around him laugh, especially new things he's never done before. Every new word he speaks makes his parents beam with pride. And when they meet other little spirits who have also just recently assumed human form, they compare their development, and the most advanced has the proudest parents.

Sometimes their pride has little to do with actual abilities. The outward appearance of a little spirit in human form seems to be of great importance, and it especially makes female humans squeal with joy. The little spirit noticed early on that his outward appearance doesn't trigger as much delight as the physical appearance of other children. His parents always get a little embarrassed when it comes to his appearance. He still has practically no hair, and his ears are really big. His parents' insecurities carry over to him, and he's just as embarrassed that he has too little hair and that his parents don't like his ears—and he dearly hopes it won't stay that way. At least, he doesn't seem to be overwhelmingly fat. One of the children on the playground is chubbier than everybody else, and his parents have a really hard time explaining that fact over and over again.

The little spirit wonders whether parents like their children less if they don't look exactly as they'd like them to. This idea confuses him. In heaven they were all the same, and the Mother Spirit made no distinctions. He quickly pushes this sad thought aside. His parents love him—he can feel that. And he'll find another way to make them proud. He learns faster than most of the others, and his parents' delight in his progress helps them forget his big ears and bald head for a moment.

Of course, his parents and the other children's parents don't call him "little spirit." That wouldn't make sense, since they were all little spirits, which some of them have, of course, temporarily forgotten. Actually, most of the children still remember, but all the grownups seem to have forgotten.

The little spirit is now called Paul. He really likes his name. He remembers how one little spirit in heaven talked about his journey and how his parents had given him the wrong name. Because of this, the other children laughed at him, which made his early years on earth very sad. But unlike our little spirit, he was lucky enough to have thick black curls and an extraordinarily straight nose, so that in spite of his name, female human children with golden hair soon gathered around him. He is one of those who report about their time on earth with great joy!

So the little spirit's name is now Paul. Nobody laughs at him because of this name, and there's even another Paul in his kindergarten, which makes him feel good. One girl comes from a faraway land and has a name that's difficult to pronounce, which causes some laughter. But Paul thinks she's very pretty, and he can already tell that she'll have the same experience as the little spirit with the soft, black curls. Different people constantly ask Paul his name, his age, and what his parents do for a living. He knows his name and age, and even his parents' professions, though he keeps pronouncing them wrong and has no idea what they mean. But he can tell it's important to know these things. That's the only way people can know who they're dealing with.

He also gets weighed and measured. He's glad that he's about the same weight and height as most of the other boys in his kindergarten. Almost all the girls are shorter than the boys, but one boy is even smaller than the girls, which means he often gets pushed around and sometimes even beaten. But not as badly as the chubby boy whose parents always give him huge cold-cut sandwiches for lunch. Oh, how he suffers! The other children have even made up special songs about him, and they never grow tired of singing them. Paul sings along, happy that he's a normal size. He doesn't feel quite comfortable doing it, but he's afraid that if he doesn't join in, the focus will be on him.

At times like these, he sometimes recalls his former home, where everyone was treated the same. But it's been a long time since he last spoke with the Mother Spirit. His earthly mother has taken her place, and because she's always present, there seems to be no more room for the Mother Spirit. Paul even feels silly now when he hears the Mother Spirit's voice now and again—that's something for little children and dreamers. He wants to be more rational than that. But as the Mother Spirit promised him, she's never far away, and as much as Paul might try to not listen, he can never completely tune out her voice. And in the few honest moments that Paul keeps to himself, he thinks the chubby boy is actually much nicer than the loudmouthed ringleader and that he would much rather play with him. And sometimes he also finds the girls more pleasant, and so sweet and peaceful that he'd prefer to surround himself with them. But he'd rather cut out his tongue than say that aloud.

And then he falls in love. This intensity he's never known before, these bolts of lightning that shoot through his body—oh, how wonderful it is to be human! She is a young lady and his teacher—his first teacher—and she has the merriest eyes and the most beautiful legs he's ever seen. She likes to show them off in short skirts, and Paul can never gaze at her enough. He thinks of nothing else, day and night. Everything else fades into the background. Nothing else is important any longer. He feels alive and electric.

Whenever he sees her, he gets all choked up, and his heart starts pounding so hard and fast he thinks people can see it through his shirt. A lot of the other boys have also fallen in love with the young lady, and even the girls are in love with her. They all rave about her and go out of their way to please her. But no one loves her as much as Paul. Whenever she praises him, Paul's world is full of sunshine, but when she scolds him or is disappointed—disappointed, that's the worst!—then the sky is covered with clouds, and his little boy's heart aches and shrouds itself in sadness.

Oh, the constant battle to gain her favor! Paul knows that he can only achieve this by good performance in school, so he studies as much as he can. At night when he closes his eyes, he can see her face, and in the morning, he can't wait to go to school. The young lady is very nice to him. He is a good student, which makes her happy. Paul loves to see her face beam, and he imagines a life with the young lady at his side. Paul is happy and feels like he's in heaven.

Until the day that everything changes. The day Paul does especially well, and the young lady rewards him with a particularly charming smile. The day he comes out of the school building and sees how the young lady is met by a man. And that man kisses her on the lips. On the lips—in public! Right in front of Paul and whoever else is walking by. The lips he has dreamt of kissing so many nights… the lips he has been gazing at every day and knows so well! And as if that weren't enough, the young lady's cheeks blush, and her eyes shine in a way that Paul has never seen before. A pain runs through his body, threatening to tear him apart. A previously unknown sense of helplessness washes over him. And he was so sure he knew her better than everyone else, that they were connected by an inseparable bond, invisible to others and never acknowledged out loud—but still not less real!

Paul feels betrayed. The world around him is falling apart. She doesn't even look back at him when she gets in the car, laughing. She doesn't care about Paul.

And she falls and falls and falls—from a once divine being to everything that fills Paul with disgust.

Paul changes. Disappointments and defeats in his life are mounting up. There's no more joy in his face. He's listless and often bitter. He becomes more and more withdrawn. Everything he does seems forced. It's been a long time since he's thought about oceans, mountains, and lakes at all, and whenever he thinks of the young lady, it's only with malice. He's getting older and more cynical. He doesn't want to listen to anybody and feels that no one understands him. He takes his bitterness out on others. His aggressiveness scares them, so they make him their leader, but that doesn't satisfy him, either. He keeps growing and growing. He hates his appearance and finds himself absurd-looking and ugly. He has sparse, ridiculous stubble, like the weaklings he's always despised. He doesn't have much hair on his head—still. His feet and hands are overly large, and they stink. The smell of sweat and cigarettes constantly clings to him.

Alcohol and drugs are also doing their part. They send him to the heights of ecstasy only to destroy him afterwards. He's ashamed. His condition shifts from intoxication and deliriousness to shame and a mind-numbing angst. He can't handle it anymore. He can't breathe. He feels abandoned and alone. He tries several times to pull himself out of the swamp by his own bootstraps, but he's just not strong enough, so his demons keep throwing him back out into the icy cold, where he feels nothing but loneliness, fear, and horror.

He masturbates a lot. Actually, he barely does anything else. His room is full of magazines of naked women in various poses, and they never fail to arouse him. A constant bittersweet smell lingers in his room. He's not popular with the girls. While the boys admire him for his crudeness, the girls find his thin hair and pale, waxy skin repulsive. They find him disgusting. He knows it. Still, he can always find someone to go out with. How he despises them for that! And he lets them feel his contempt—he knows how to destroy.

In the schoolyard, he sometimes notices girls who are very different from anything he knows. They're pretty and have long, clean hair, and they're self-confident and exude the lightheartedness of spring. When he sees these girls laughing and swinging their pretty little hips as they sashay across the schoolyard, the spark from another life touches him—a life that is bright, pure, and carefree. And he gets an urgent desire to break out of his cocoon, to escape the darkness and the suffocation, to breathe in vastness and freedom. But he quickly cuts off those thoughts again. It's clear these girls are not interested in him, that he doesn't belong in their radiant, beautiful lives. They're popular and go out with boys who drive their fathers' cars. They view him only with contempt, but most of the time they don't even so much as look at him. They simply ignore him. In moments like that, memories of his first teacher flash across his mind, but that feels like a lifetime ago.

The more Paul feels their rejection, the more he despises the girls he sleeps with. They're not pure and affluent but just as dirty as he is—just as needy, just as broken. He humiliates and insults them. He enjoys seeing them suffer. In his more honest moments, he has to admit that it's really himself he hates—his face in the mirror, the constant rejection, the urge to torment himself and others, his inability to break out of it. But there are also moments when, through the haze that covers his life, he catches a glimpse of freedom and openness.

At least, he's managed to resist his parents' and teachers' constant dictates, to resist the pressure to perform and succeed—a pressure that sometimes threatened to strangle him. Deep in his heart, he wants to be loved for who he is and not for what he represents. A profound longing for this kind of unconditional love awakens in him and keeps getting stronger and stronger. It's a longing he feels most urgently and painfully when he looks up at the starlit night sky. In those moments, it's as though a voice is speaking to him, a loving voice that he'd almost forgotten and that brings tears to his eyes.

Gradually, Paul calms down. It gets too exhausting to live in a constant state of struggle, and he no longer feels like fighting anymore. His body has also finally settled down and resumed its normal proportions. His hair will always be sparse—there's nothing he can do about that. And his ears are still huge. But his hands and feet are now the right size for his body, his skin is free of blemishes, his facial hair is no longer scruffy, and though he still indulges in erotic fantasies, his life no longer revolves around them. He has made peace with himself and can now meet others with genuine affection. From time to time he falls in love, and though he still has to learn how to deal with rejection, every now and again he's lucky, and his feelings are reciprocated. He's still not the kind of guy who attracts the most popular girls, but his life doesn't seem hopeless anymore.

Paul finishes school and moves to another town to begin his study of human sciences. That means that he occupies himself with matters of human existence. He often recognizes himself in the most profound questions, and he increasingly starts to sense a feeling of unfulfillment inside, a restlessness that he wants to satisfy. His intuition tells him he can only find the answers within himself.

When he was a child, his parents often took him to a house of worship, but prayer always remained somewhat abstract for him. Now he wants to embark on this path again to see if it maybe holds the answers to his questions. So he goes to his childhood house of worship and speaks to the saints who are worshipped there. He also seeks counsel in the prayerbooks, and he finds a certain peace in these surroundings. For the last few years, he has dearly missed his moments of silence, which is why he now deeply enjoys and cherishes them. But just as in his childhood, prayer remains fruitless for him, and it's hard for him to believe that his prayers have power. Besides, he doesn't like all the dogma and the rules that have been laid down here. They seem outdated and sometimes even inhumane.

As time goes by, he visits different places of worship from other faiths, but nowhere can he find a satisfying answer to his questions—those nagging questions that he himself can hardly put into words. But even if not one single religion is able to answer his question, there is one thing he finds in all the different movements: a core, common to all, with no theoretical approach or complex implementation. This core holds all the characteristics of love. It speaks of eternity and happiness, of joy, hope, and trust. Paul senses that he's on the right track and that he can use aspects of all the different doctrines to arrive at this core, which holds so much promise in itself and triggers a deep yearning in him. When he delves deeper into the subject, he learns that many authors over the millennia have addressed his exact questions and have tried to provide answers. The words of some of them touch him powerfully and stir his longing for truth so deeply that he feels they were the work of wise men. These moments are sacred to him. At those times, he feels such a deep peace inside, such a freedom and boundlessness, that he wants to hold onto them forever.

But as unexpectedly as these moments come, they vanish just as quickly. This leaves him in despair. Just as he used to run after drugs and alcohol, he now longs for these rare sacred moments. He reads every book he can find on the subject, but at some point he's no longer content to depend on other peoples' words. He senses that true peace lies somewhere deep within him, that it's the core of his being, a spark from the eternal fire to which so many different names have been given. But human symbols can only hint at its greatness, yet never fully express it. Just as the eye cannot see itself, so the origin of all things can only be vaguely described. Its full glory can only be directly experienced.

Meanwhile Paul has once again found his love for the mountains and lakes, and since he feels closest to his core in nature, he grabs a backpack and sets out on a journey to himself. He travels through mountains and crosses oceans. He learns about foreign countries, customs, and traditions. He is alone and experiences solitude. He meets people and discusses things with them. He begins to practice yoga and to meditate, which helps him to calm his thoughts. Behind all the storms of human emotion, he then feels the eternal spark within himself.

It was for these moments that he set out on his trip. Deep within himself, he finds a place where past and future no longer play a role—where a voice speaks to him, a voice so often drowned out by everyday life. But if you listen carefully, you can hear within it the sound of pure love. It speaks of joy, of freedom and happiness, and it bestows comfort and hope. It knows no condemnation and no guilt. It is understanding and compassion, and it surrounds Paul with the warm embrace of a loving mother. Paul knows that everyday life will take over again, but nothing will ever be the same. For now he's sure this voice is inside him, that he can listen to its kindly sound whenever he feels the need for the unfathomable yet ever-present magic of infinite love. He decides to frequently wrap himself in this love, to live a life free from doubt, judgment, and insecurity—a life filled with a wonderful childlike trust.

Paul returns to the city and resumes his studies. The questions he had no longer burn within him, and he has found a new peace inside that helps him to deal with the hills and valleys of his life with more serenity. He graduates with honors and becomes a teacher. He enjoys teaching, and his students like him. He also meets and falls in love with a nice lady, with whom he shares the desire to have a family. It's not the same urgent love he felt before, but it combines deep friendship with mutual respect, which both of them consider a good basis for a life together. Paul wants to leave the still palpable years of guilt and physicality behind, and his love for this woman is like a cleansing. She, on the other hand, wants to fulfill her vision of a happy family. She's known it was what she wanted since she was a little girl.

They get married, and Paul will always hold their wedding day as a pleasant memory—the minister's speech, the weather—everything showed its best side. They go on their honeymoon, get to know each other a bit better, and enjoy their time together. As soon as they come back, they move into a nice home just outside the city. Paul's job pays well, and he can provide them with a comfortable, risk-free life. They can't afford a lot of luxuries, but those aren't needed anyway. And he certainly makes enough for their yearly vacation and a small car. They build a circle of friends with whom they share their interests, and they spend pleasant and enjoyable times together.

In his quieter moments, Paul wonders whether he really wants to continue living like this forever. The routine of his life seems to overwhelm him more and more, and it awakens in him a sense of missed opportunities—like a steel clamp that wraps itself around his neck and tightens more and more until it threatens to choke him. Then he longingly thinks back to the heated discussions he had with his fellow travelers on the quest for meaning. He thinks back to the mountains and lakes that hold within themselves the promise of the still unexplored… to the new horizons he strove toward with such urgent and tireless, even relentless, energy— questions he chewed on till he found the answers. And though these were uncomfortable times, full of doubt and detours on the search for meaning, in retrospect, he never felt so alive again. Back then he wanted the routine that now made his life so pleasant and predictable, a life pursued by every citizen. But now he feels that his inner flame, nourished by curiosity, adventure, and a lust for life, is becoming a feeble little flicker, in danger of being extinguished and taking all the magic with it.

But before his doubt threatens to destroy the comfort of the familiar and the lives of those around him, its merciless tongue is curbed and repressed. Reason steps forward and declares his dreams irrational and thus not desirable. Paul believes it and is ashamed he allowed himself to have such immature and selfish desires. He submits to his everyday life and tries to feel gratitude.

His life with his wife, though based on mutual love and respect, is not always easy. She has a hard time believing she's worthy of love. She was raised with the objective of pleasing others and meeting their expectations to the point of self-sacrifice. Led by the needs of others, she tries to find joy in her heart, while at the same time she quickly moves away from what her heart desires. All her bustling serves the single purpose of earning lasting love and appreciation from other people—a hopeless and debilitating endeavor. But she does it anyway, over and over again. Whether from friends, family, or strangers, as soon as she encounters rejection, anger, or any other type of discord, her carefully constructed self-assurance crumbles like a house of cards. Then she blames herself—or others. For her, everything is a matter of guilt, and hers has grown so large over time that she finds herself in a desperate cycle of blame and remorse. She is consumed by self-doubt, which poisons her being and makes it difficult for her to feel peace of mind and joy.

Paul tries to convey to her what he's learned on his journeys. He knows that the same spark that illumines his being shines in her as well. He sees it often. When for brief unguarded moments she sheds her cares, he can see in her the young girl she could have been and still could be—without yesterday or tomorrow, without guilt or remorse—in the here and now, full of life and joy, delighting in the freshness of perpetual renewal. But it's difficult for him to convince her of her worth. She tells him to be reasonable and realistic—life is not that easy! They should be glad to have found each other and be healthy. There's not much more you can expect from life. Anything else would be presumptuous and ungrateful. Paul doesn't know how to make her understand that he is grateful—very grateful. But he craves a life of lightheartedness, one that attracts the sunny side and the best, the unexpected... one that expects the impossible, a life of adventure—not always easy, sometimes sad and with hurdles to cross, but infused with a deep joy and guided by the still voice within that always whispers to him.

These are the things he tries to explain to her, but she won't hear him. She would definitely feel better if they had children, which is her purpose, and after all, she's not getting any younger. Paul would love to have children, and his wife's sudden newly awakened sexuality makes him very happy. She is not like the women in the magazines from his youth, and she's also not like the girls on his journey, who explored with him what till then he'd left unexplored. But his vivid imagination and memory give him a boost, and in spite of his wife's prudishness, he enjoys their intimacy.

She soon gets pregnant and gives birth to a daughter. The birth is long and difficult, and Paul empathizes with his wife, who is going through severe pain. Their daughter is a healthy and beautiful baby girl, but Paul secretly wonders if his daughter isn't maybe a little too chubby—other girls are skinnier than she is. But he loves her from the bottom of his heart and cannot stop looking at her. She's so carefree—she only wants her most basic needs met, which of course happens promptly. And there's something else, too—almost a kind of wisdom, as though she knew something her parents had no access to. Sometimes Paul gets the impression that she's the adult and he's the child. He tries to remember the time when he, too, was that small, but of course he can't remember it anymore. Did he, too, have this calm wisdom and contentment in his eyes? His parents never mentioned it to him.

The girl is thriving beautifully, and to Paul's relief, she grows at a rapid pace and is soon as thin as a rail. If you ask Paul, it's much too soon, but his wife gets pregnant a second time, and this time she gives birth to a little boy, her pride and joy.

The birth of the two children leaves a powerful mark on the mother's psyche. She is now increasingly overwhelmed and no longer knows how to please everyone. Feelings of guilt lead to stress and eat at her. She takes medicine to meet life's challenges. More and more, she is stricken by panic attacks and breaks into a sweat. She's reluctant to go out, and she hides herself away. She and Paul no longer see their friends—it's just all too much for her. The panic attacks become stronger and more frequent, and she's soon living in a state of constant anxiety. On top of that, the demons from her past awaken. They stem from her earliest childhood, and she has tried to suppress them all her life. But now they're resurfacing, and they won't allow her to push them down anymore.

The family is helpless. They have no idea what this is all about. Even now, after all these years, the mother cannot and will not talk about what she experienced back then. Instead, she gets more and more silent, until she finally stops talking at all, cut off and alone in her fear and darkness. Paul and the children can no longer help her. They, too, are overwhelmed by her illness. Finally, they take the mother to a hospital, where she'll be staying for a while.

Every Sunday, the family goes to visit the mother, and each time she's so happy to see them. They bring her chocolates and flowers and stay as long as they can. Paul always looks at her with great tenderness—she's so vulnerable and so afraid. How he would love to drive away the demons of her past and see the spark within her shining brightly again, so he could live a life of joy with her and the children. He doesn't believe she can be cured in the hospital, but he sees no other option. Deep in his heart, he still hopes his wife will one day be able to leave the hospital so that both of them will finally be able to live the life they've always wanted—not the wild, driven life of his youth, which he sometimes still feels flaring up inside, but the calm and peaceful life that has become their common play.

The children are suffering. Oh, how ashamed they are at school that their mother is in a mental hospital! At first, they want to keep it a secret, so they invent different stories to explain their mother's long absence. But these are soon exposed as lies, and the children become victims of cruel mockery. They love their mother very much, but sometimes they also hate her for her weakness and their father for his soft, almost feminine ways. Why couldn't he have chosen a strong woman, one full of energy and joy, with an infectious laugh, who makes the most delicious sandwiches for lunch, and whom they could introduce to their friends with pride? But, no, he had to seek out a weak woman, one who would never really be able to function again, even if she were ever released from the hospital. On top of that, her face is puffy from the medicine, and it looks gray and sallow. Her hair is turning gray, and since she doesn't take care of herself, she looks much older than she actually is.

On the rare occasions when she goes out among people and swaps her yoga pants for the same old-fashioned clothing, the children beg that their few remaining friends should not see their mother like this. It's been a long time since Paul and his wife had any friends, so he spends a lonely life by himself with the children.

The children's early years are difficult, which temporarily breaks the monotonous lethargy. The son loves his mother dearly, and he has a hard time coping with her condition. He's sure his mother is not this tired, broken creature he sees every Sunday—oh, how he dreads these visits!—but that there's a beautiful flower blossoming deep beneath her sallow skin. This is at least how he sees her in his dreams. As painful as she is to look at, he loves her delicate hands and the way she gently raises the corners of her mouth when she smiles at him. And sometimes, on rare occasions—though he has seen it—she has a twinkle in her eye, as if she wants to let him know that deep beneath the sadness and the pain, there still lives the same person who once whirled him in the air and nursed him.

The son feels that he's at fault. Didn't she fall ill after his birth, right around the time he selfishly nursed at her breast? He feels he must have done something wrong or broken something for her to become like this. Doesn't his father always say it was after the birth of the second child that things went downhill with her, that she couldn't handle the pressure anymore? The son doesn't talk about it to anyone, but the guilt weighs heavily upon him. And it breaks his heart when his friends laugh at his mother and call her names that make him feel all choked up with sadness and anger. Sometimes he just can't help it. Because of this, he often lashes out at those who offend his mother, and his tender heart hardens. From now on, he won't let anyone or anything get near his wounded heart. He'll never let anyone hurt him again. He feels incredibly lonely.

The daughter accepts her mother's illness, and she admires and loves her father, who constantly takes care of her and her brother with such humility and devotion. But it hurts her to see him so quiet and withdrawn much of the time. She tries to capture her father's love and attention, and she does her best to help him and to make all their lives as nice as possible. She tries to replace her mother by doing the household chores and managing the expenses. But he doesn't seem to notice. She puts flowers on the table and hangs pictures on the walls. She plays music to cheer him up, but all her efforts go unheeded. It's not that Paul doesn't love his daughter and doesn't find her behavior touching, but he's retreated into his shell, where he can't bother anyone. He thinks his daughter is driven by a sense of duty, and he doesn't want to be a burden on anyone, like his wife.

The more he secludes himself, the more forcefully and desperately his daughter fights for a normal life for them all, one that does not fall victim to her mother's illness. To make her father proud, she buries herself in her books—maybe academic success is the way to his heart. And she becomes the best in her class. Her father is in fact very proud to have such a talented daughter, and her achievements confirm even more that the right response is to leave her alone and not get in her way. Meanwhile, he doesn't notice how he leaves his daughter to her pain and helplessness—the helplessness of never being able to heal the wounds inflicted by her mother's illness and the pain of not being good enough in her father's eyes, no matter what she does.

Thus the years go by. Just like Paul, the son becomes softer and gentler after his teenage years, and instead of closing himself off because of his mother's illness, he decides to become a doctor so he can understand it. In the future, he also wants to be in a position to help people in similar situations. While in college, he falls in love with a very pretty young woman, whom he eventually marries. She is full of optimism and joy and makes his heart beat faster every time he looks at her. She visits his mother with him on Sundays and treats the sick woman with so much love and understanding that he knows beyond all doubt he has the right woman at his side.

His sister, too, now a successful attorney who devotes her considerable energies to the less privileged, has also finally found a partner with whom she can be herself. After a long and tireless courtship, he is finally able to persuade the initially reluctant and suspicious girl with his calm and trusting nature. And although he can't keep up with her inexhaustible energy, he still provides her with a calm and dependable haven and loves her just the way she is.

The whole family gathers to celebrate after the son's final exams. Even the mother is given leave from the hospital for the day, and although she doesn't say much, she looks pretty and happy. Her demons seem to have vanished, and she exudes an almost solemn tranquility. For the first time in years, the family feels united and almost carefree again.

The children are now earning their own money and are passionately determined to give their father a better life. They buy him a small, cozy house right around the corner. That way they can come by every day and look after him.

Several years have elapsed. Paul has again begun to pursue his hobbies and is slowly coming out of his shell. But if he looks deep into his heart, he realizes that he misses his wife, his lifelong partner. Even the daily visits of his children can't change that. His children sense this longing in him as he sits in his garden under the shade of a cherry tree—his favorite tree—sits and gazes into the distance, pondering what might have been.

And so the son heads off to his mother's hospital, speaks to the director, and is allowed to bring his mother home—to a new home but to the familiar arms of the one who's always loved her and who has stood by her side as a lifelong friend. It's supposed to be a surprise. The daughter sets up an extra room for the mother, where she can retreat to should life outside the hospital become too stressful.

The surprise is a complete success, and the welcome is both overwhelming and calm. Paul and his wife come together in an intimate embrace, and looking deep into each other's eyes, they understand each other without words. She now senses he was right when he wanted to reveal to her the joy and the lightness of being. For the first time, he's able to comprehend her pain and horror, and for a moment he can feel, deep within his own heart, the demons that have tormented his spouse for so long. He then takes her by the hand and leads her slowly into the garden. He takes the lawn chair, places pillows and blankets on it, and makes a bed for her under the shade of the blossoming cherry tree. Her slight smile and a subtle twinkle in her eyes make his heart overflow with tenderness, and he realizes for the first time that he has no regrets. Life hasn't always been easy for him, but the love never went out of it. He thinks he remembers, a long, long time ago, that a beautiful voice once told him something about love. He doesn't remember what it was, but he's sure it was important.

The children are standing in the garden, watching the silent interaction. And in them, too, a change begins to take place. The son understands he's not responsible for his mother's illness. He sees that no child could carry such a far-reaching responsibility and that fate often seeks its way without first asking for approval. People sometimes need to practice the art of accepting circumstances without judgment and without carrying the burden of guilt for a lifetime. And the ability to love themselves greatly helps to accept even the incomprehensible.

The son looks over at his beautiful, happy wife, perceiving her as a single affirmation of life, though she, too, has gone through difficult times, sometimes with seemingly insurmountable obstacles. He lovingly takes her by the hand and winks at her. They'll go make babies now—he has to make sure the beauty he's holding by the hand, and for which he's so grateful, will be passed onto someone!

The daughter and her husband are also watching the scene that's playing out between the parents. The daughter knows deep down that she and her husband will be bound together by a lifelong friendship. They already understand each other without needing to say much, and they feel that their souls vibrate in harmony. She has to smile when she looks back on how she wanted to please her father. She sees now that for too long she remained a little girl, yearning for love and attention in a place where pain and disappointment prevailed. Desperate, she harbored expectations of her father that he was in no position to fulfill. But instead of seeing his pain and weakness, she was convinced that she saw her own worthlessness in his rejection. Only the man at her side had shown her that she didn't need to be anything other than exactly what she already was.

So the children and their partners leave the garden. Paul has also been watching his children, and his heart overflows with love and pride, mixed with a drop of sadness over missed opportunities. But he senses that many more opportunities lie ahead, and he sits down on a lawn chair next to his wife and takes her hand in his.

The next few weeks go by peacefully and slowly, imbued with the magic of spring. Paul and his wife spend most of their time in the garden under the shade of the cherry tree, listening to the humming of the bees. They don't talk much, and his wife says nothing at all. But she exudes a calmness Paul has never felt in her before. He knows that she's finally driven away the demons of her past, and he respects that she doesn't want to destroy this newfound peace with words. He also doesn't say much, but sometimes he tells her about the years without her, about his loneliness, his desperation, and his sorrow for never having shown her the full extent of his love. Then she gently squeezes his hand and they nod almost imperceptibly at each other, knowing they were always more connected than separated.

Eventually the days grow cooler, and they have to withdraw to the house. They light the furnace and sit on their chairs before the fire, snuggled in blankets, watching the flames together in silence. As the leaves fall from the trees, Paul observes that his soul is beginning to separate from his body. For a long time, he's had a tumor that slowly but steadily has been eating away at him from the inside, and he feels he won't be able to withstand it much longer. He's never mentioned anything to his family, but now he knows it's time to tell his wife. So one evening he tells her about his illness, and when she holds his hand, as she does every night, for the first time, he feels a faint trembling. They look at each other, and he sees a tear trickling down her cheek. He takes it with his finger and touches it to his lips. She smiles at him, full of love, and her eyes ask the question that has tormented him for so long.

"Yes," he says, "yes, I'm scared—I'm scared beyond imagination. I'm scared of not being able to breathe. I'm scared that there's no coming back. But most of all, I'm scared of the loneliness and emptiness when everything is over. I'm so scared that sometimes I feel like my heart will stop even before the illness has a chance to kill me. And I'm scared I'll no longer feel love in the void, that I'll just disappear—forget you, our life—that I'll simply be obliterated. I'm so scared, and that fear is so lonely."

And he starts to cry. It's the first time he's ever cried in front of his wife. She slowly pulls him closer, and they embrace each other. They hold each other for a long time, as only two people who love each other can do, and she gives him a feeling of comfort.

In the days that follow, Paul talks a lot about his fear, his sleepless nights, the nightmares, but also about other dreams. Sometimes in his sleep he sees a landscape more beautiful than any he's ever seen before. He can feel a love so strong and deep it surpasses anything imaginable. It fills his heart and his whole being and is so unimaginably beautiful that he's disappointed when he awakens. He feels guilty when he admits this feeling to his wife, but she just smiles and nods understandingly.

Sometimes he also hears a voice, one he believes has been with him all his life, but never as clearly as lately. It's incredibly beautiful—so familiar and more beautiful than anything he's ever heard. And it tells him to not be afraid, that it's time for him to come home. He would love to believe that voice, but in his waking moments, when his reason kicks in, he's afraid of the unknown, the darkness, the void. And his wife listens to him and nods, and he has the feeling that she understands completely and that she experienced the same fears many years earlier during the painful years of her lonely illness. And sometimes she tilts her head to the side in her special way, and a quiet smile plays around her lips. In these moments he is sure that she, too, can hear the voice and that it's this voice that she listens to with such devout attention when she's not listening to her husband's beloved voice.

For all his fears, Paul is grateful that fate has given him the opportunity to prepare his children for his approaching death. He calls them together and breaks the news to them. They cry a lot. The son blames himself for not being able to help him as a doctor, and the daughter feels she wasn't good and grateful enough during his life. But they soon recognize the old patterns that brought them so many years of pain, and for these remaining hours they resolve not to repeat their old mistakes but to spend these last moments in love and gratitude for the good they have received. They tell each other stories, hold hands, laugh and cry a lot. Paul now has the opportunity and the courage to finally tell his children about his boundless love for them, and the second he sees himself regretting that he didn't do it sooner, he stops, reconsiders, and is happy and grateful for the chance to do so now. He also tells them about his fear, but more about his hope. And he promises to keep a watchful eye on them from eternity—and on his grandson, who is growing in his daughter's womb and will be named Paul. A beautiful name—on that they all agree. At some point, they all become exhausted, and the children stand up and say goodbye. They give their father a long hug, full of love—there's nothing more to be said. Then they leave, and he sits down next to his wife. He takes her hand, and as the last leaf falls from the trees, he goes to sleep.

"Welcome home, little spirit! How did you like your adventure?"

The little spirit rubs his eyes. He is still perplexed. "How long have I been gone?" he asks, and then adds, slightly upset: "I did not have the feeling you were with me the whole time. Sometimes, I was able to hear your voice, but often enough you left me alone with my pain." He's so glad to be back home—the journey has worn him out.

The Mother Spirit laughs. "You went down just a little while ago, little spirit. For us here, no time has passed at all. And I was always with you. But to experience human existence, you also had to learn about pain. Believe me, though, I held you fast in my arms in your sleep and kissed your forehead. With every breath you took, you communicated with me, but like so many people, you preferred to ignore my voice. Rest now, little spirit, you have been in human form for a long time—it must have worn you out. Don't worry. I will watch your family down there while you rest."

"Bah!" the little spirit retorts. "I'll do that myself. Look, Mother Spirit! My grandson is just being born down there! I'll do him a favor and give him small ears. You really could have spared me that nasty little trick. Those ears didn't make my time as a human being any easier. And not even enough hair to cover them…"

Then he looks down at his beloved family and his little grandchild. He senses that his wife's little spirit will soon also be coming home and leaving only her faded body on earth. He's looking forward to the reunion. And he's already thinking about what he could do better when he returns to earth—probably try to hear the Mother Spirit's voice more often. That would have spared him many lonely moments.

And he says: "How beautiful this journey could have been had I not forgotten you and your boundless love, Mother Spirit!" I was constantly struggling to compete and keep up with your other children, and I completely forgot that I wanted to love and enjoy the mountains, the lakes, and the beauty of the earth." And the little spirit wistfully looks down on the other little spirits who are still allowed to live on earth and who make their lives so difficult, though they could be so beautiful.

"Mother Spirit, are you going to let me go down there again?" he asks, as his eyes already begin to close. "I still have so much to learn, and I've grown so fond of humans. It's true that they're a little crazy, as I first thought, but their love can work miracles. You said that humans call us 'Love.' Thank you for giving me the chance to see myself through their eyes." And with that, he falls asleep.

"Sleep well, little spirit," says the Mother Spirit and takes him tenderly in her arms. Meanwhile, the Mother Spirit keeps a constant watchful eye on the little family below on earth.

The Author

I was born in 1973 in Breslau, Poland, and grew up in Germany. I studied law at Heinrich-Heine University in Düsseldorf, and after my legal clerkship, I received my doctorate in media and competition law from the University of Münster. I subsequently became interested in business, studied at Stanford Graduate School of Business in California, and co-founded the global online donation platform ammado.

I'm a very passionate person and interested in all sorts of things, such a reading, hiking, skiing, socializing, yoga, and technology. Having spent many years in Dublin, Ireland, I now live in Zürich, Switzerland, where I dearly enjoy the beauty of the country's lakes and mountains.

My sincerest "thank you" for reading the story. I hope you enjoyed it, and I would love to hear from you!

Yours, Anna

anna.camilla.kupka@gmail.com

The Illustrator

I've been working as a commercial artist, illustrator, and designer for more than 25 years. I'm also a painter who never tires of creating my own dreamscapes in oil, acrylic, and watercolor. Born in the Rhine region of Germany, my restless spirit finally found its home in Bavaria, between dark forests, clear blue skies, and majestic mountains—the right place to be inspired by the master hand of nature.

Live, breathe, paint!

Sylivia Gruber
www.en.gruber-art.de

46753402R00038

Made in the USA
Lexington, KY
14 November 2015